credits

Photographer • Jarek Duk
Art Direction & Styling • Georgina Brant
Design Layout • Quail Studio
Model • Carime

First published in Great Britain in 2020 by
Quail Publishing Limited
Old Town Hall, Market Square, Buckingham, Buckinghamshire, MK18 1NJ
E-mail: info@quailstudio.co.uk

Classic Tweed Style
EAN: 978-1-9162445-3-5

collection

short version

tweed jacket · pattern pg 22

long version

tweed jacket · pattern pg 22

houndstooth jacket · pattern pg 28

herringbone scarf · pattern pg 34

beanie · pattern pg 36

snood · pattern pg 38

roll neck jumper · pattern pg 40

cable detail jumper · pattern pg 44

tweed
jacket

quail studio

Short Version

Long Version

houndstooth
jacket

quail studio

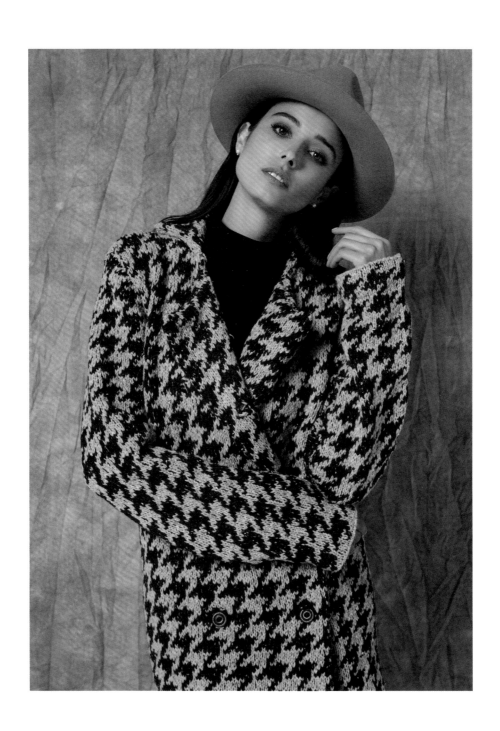

herringbone
scarf

quail studio

beanie

quail studio

snood

quail studio

roll neck
jumper

quail studio

cable detail
jumper

quail studio

patterns

tweed jacket ...

 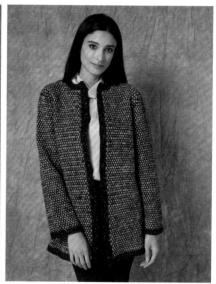

SIZE

To fit bust

71-76	81-86	91-97	102-107	112-117	122-127	cm
28-30	32-34	36-38	40-42	44-46	48-50	in

Actual Size

90	100	110	120	130	140	cm
35½	39¼	43¼	47¼	51¼	55	in

YARN

Rowan Valley Tweed

Short Jacket
A - Gordale 105

4	5	5	6	6	6	x 50gm

B - Malham 101

4	4	5	5	6	6	x 50gm

C - Penyghent 104

4	4	5	5	6	6	x 50gm

Long Jacket
A - Gordale 105

5	5	5	6	6	7	x 50gm

B - Malham 101

4	5	5	6	6	7	x 50gm

C - Penyghent 104

4	5	5	6	6	7	x 50gm

NEEDLES

4.5mm (no 7) (US 7) circular needles at least 80(80,100,100, 120,120)cm long

TENSION

24 stitches and 22.5 rows to 10cm / 4in measured over pattern using 4½mm (US 7) needles and holding 2 strands of yarn together.

EXTRAS

Stitch Holders

SHORT JACKET
BACK AND FRONTS
Knitted in one piece to armhole shaping.
Using 4.5mm (US 7) needles and holding 2 strands of yarn A together, cast on 197(220,243,266,289,312) sts.
Piece is worked flat. If using circular needle, do not join in the round.
Work in g st for 2cm, ending with a RS row.
Next Row (WS): K17(20,22,19,21,23), K in front and back of next st, * K17(17,17,18,18,18), K in front and back of next st, rep from * to last 17(19,22,18,20,22) sts, K to end. 207(231,255,279,303,327) sts.

Work pattern:
Row 1 (RS): Holding 2 strands of yarn A together, K2, * yarn to front, sl1 P wise, yarn back, K1, rep from * to last 3 sts, yarn to front, sl1 P wise, yarn back, K2.
Row 2: Holding 2 strands of yarn B together, K1, with yarn at back, sl1 P wise, yarn to front, P1, * yarn to back, sl1 P wise, yarn to front, P1, rep from * to last 2 sts, yarn to back, sl1 P wise, K1.
Row 3: Holding 2 strands of yarn C together, K2, * yarn to front, sl1 P wise, yarn back, K1, rep from * to last 3 sts, yarn to front, sl1 P wise, yarn back, K2.
Row 4: Holding 2 strands of yarn A together, K1, with yarn at back, sl1 P wise, yarn to front, P1, * yarn to back, sl1 P wise, yarn to front, P1, rep from * to last 2 sts, yarn to back, sl1 P wise, K1.
Row 5: Holding 2 strands of yarn B together, K2, * yarn to front, sl1 P wise, yarn back, K1, rep from * to last 3 sts, yarn to front, sl1 P wise, yarn back, K2.
Row 6: Holding 2 strands of yarn C together, K1, with yarn at back, sl1 P wise, yarn to front, P1, * yarn to back, sl1 P wise, yarn to front, P1, rep from * to last 2 sts, yarn to back, sl1 P wise, K1.
These 6 rows form patt. **
Cont in patt until work meas 37(38,39,40,41,42)cm, ending with a RS row. Make a note of which patt row you finish on for Sleeve.

*** **Shape armholes**
Next Row (WS): Patt 43(48,54,59,65,71), cast off next 13(15,15,17,17,17) sts, patt to last 56(63,69,76,82,88) sts, cast off next 13(15,15,17,17,17) sts, patt to end.

RIGHT FRONT
Row 1 (RS): Patt 41(46,52,57,63,69), K2tog, turn and work on these 42(47,53,58,64,70) sts only.
Row 2: P2tog, patt to end.
Row 3: Patt to last 2 sts, K2tog.
Rows 4-5: Rep last 2 rows once more. 38(43,49,54,60,66) sts.
Row 6: Patt to end.
Row 7: Patt to last 2 sts, K2tog.
Rep last 2 rows 4(4,5,5,6,6) times more. 33(38,43,48,53,59) sts.
Cont without shaping until armhole meas 14(15,15,16,16,17)cm, ending with a RS row.

Shape neck
Next Row (WS): Patt to last 7(7,8,8,9,9) sts, turn and slip these 7(7,8,8,9,9) sts onto st holder.
26(31,35,40,44,50) sts.
Next Row: K2tog, patt to end.
Next Row: Patt to last 2 sts, P2tog.
Rep last 2 rows 3 times more. 18(23,27,32,36,42) sts.
Cont without shaping until armhole meas 19(20,21,22,23,24)cm, ending with a RS row.

Shape shoulder
Cast off 9(11,13,16,18,21) sts at beg of next row, patt to end. 9(12,14,16,18,21) sts.
Patt 1 row. Cast off.

BACK
With RS facing, rejoin yarn to remaining sts, K2tog, patt 91(101,113,123,135,147), K2tog, turn and work on these 93(103,115,125,137,149) sts only.
Row 1: Work 2tog, patt to last 2 sts, work 2tog.
Rows 2-4: Rep last row 3 times more. 85(95,107,117,129,141) sts.
Row 5: Patt to end.
Row 6: K2tog, patt to last 2 sts, K2tog.
Rep last 2 rows 4(4,5,5,6,6) times more. 75(85,95,105,115,127) sts.
Cont without shaping until armhole meas 19(20,21,22,23,24)cm ending with a WS row.

Shape shoulders
Cont in patt, cast off 9(11,13,16,18,21) sts at beg of next 2 rows and 9(12,14,16,18,21) sts at beg of foll 2 rows. 39(39,41,41,43,43) sts.
Leave rem sts on a st holder.

LEFT FRONT
With RS facing, rejoin yarn to rem sts, K2tog and patt to end. 42(47,53,58,64,70) sts
Row 1 (WS): Patt to last 2 sts, P2tog.
Row 2: K2tog, patt to end.
Rows 3-4: Rep last 2 rows once more. 38(43,49,54,60,66) sts.
Row 5: Patt to end.
Row 6: K2tog, patt to end.
Rep last 2 rows 4(4,5,5,6,6) times more. 33(38,43,48,53,59) sts.
Cont without shaping until armhole meas 14(15,15,16,16,17)cm, ending with a WS row.

Shape neck
Next Row (RS): Patt to last 7(7,8,8,9,9) sts, turn and slip these 7(7,8,8,9,9) sts onto st holder.
26(31,35,40,44,50) sts.
Next Row: P2tog, patt to end.
Next Row: Patt to last 2 sts, K2tog.
Rep last 2 rows 3 times more. 18(23,27,32,36,42) sts.
Cont without shaping until armhole meas 19(20,21,22,23,24)cm, ending with a WS row.

Shape shoulder

Cast off 9(11,13,16,18,21) sts at beg of next row, patt to end. 9(12,14,16,18,21) sts. Patt 1 row. Cast off.

SLEEVES (both alike)

Using 4.5mm (US 7) needles and holding 2 strands of yarn A together, cast on 54(54,57,57,60,62) sts.
Work in g st for 2cm, ending with a RS row.
Next Row (WS): K5(5,7,7,6,7), K in front and back of next st, * K6(6,5,5,5,5), K in front and back of next st, rep from * to last 6(6,7,7,5,6) sts, K to end. 61(61,65,65,69,71) sts.
Work 6-row pattern as for Back and Front.
Keep pattern correct, inc 1 st at each end of next and 0(2,2,8,8,10) foll 6th rows, then on every foll 8th row to 77(81,85,89,93,97) sts.
Cont without shaping until sleeve meas 40(41,42,43,44,45)cm, ending with same RS patt row as Back before armhole shaping.

Shape top

Cast off 7(8,8,9,9,9) sts at beg of next 2 rows. 63(65,69,71,75,79) sts.
Next Row (WS): P2tog, patt to last 2 sts, P2tog. 61(63,67,69,73,77) sts.
Next Row: Patt to end.
Next Row: Patt to end.
Next Row: Patt to end.
Next Row (WS): P2tog, patt to last 2 sts, P2tog.
Next Row: Patt to end.
Rep last 2 rows 6(7,6,7,8,8) times more. 47(47,53,53,55,59) sts.
Next Row: Work 2tog, patt to last 2 sts, work 2tog.
Rep last row 5(5,7,7,7,9) times more. 35(35,37,37,39,39) sts.
Next Row: Cast off 3, patt to last 2 sts, work 2tog.
Rep last row 3 times more. 19(19,21,21,23,23) sts.
Cast off.

MAKING UP

Press as described on the information page.
Join both shoulder seams using mattress stitch.

Neckband

With RS facing, using 4.5mm (US 7) needles and holding 2 strands of yarn A together, K1(1,2,2,3,3), [K2tog, K1] twice across sts on Right Front st holder, pick up and K11(11,13,13,15,15) sts up Right Front neck edge, K3(3,5,5,6,6), K2tog, [K4, K2tog] 5 times, K4(4,4,4,5,5) across Back neck sts, pick up and K11(11,13,13,15,15) sts down Left Front neck edge, then [K1, K2tog] twice, K1(1,2,2,3,3) across sts on Left Front st holder. 65(65,73,73,81,81) sts.
Work in g st for 2cm, ending with a RS row.
Cast off.

Front bands

With RS facing, using 4.5mm (US 7) needles and holding 2 strands of yarn A together, pick up and K120(124,128,132,136,140) sts along edge of one Front.
Work in g st for 2cm, ending with a RS row.
Cast off.

Work other side to match.
Sew in sleeves.
Join sleeve seams.

LONG JACKET
BACK AND FRONTS
Work as Back and Fronts of Short Jacket to **.
Cont in pattern until work meas 57(58,59,60,61,62)cm, ending with a RS row.
Make a note of which patt row you finish on for Sleeve.
Complete as Back and Fronts of Short Jacket from *** to end.

SLEEVES (both alike)
Work as sleeves of Short Jacket.

MAKING UP
Press as described on the information page.
Join both shoulder seams using mattress stitch.
Neckband
Work Neckband as Short Jacket
Front bands
With RS facing, using 4.5mm (US 7) needles and holding 2 strands of yarn A
together, pick up and K164(168,172,176,180,184) sts along edge of one Front.
Work in g st for 2cm, ending with a RS row.
Cast off.
Work other side to match.
Sew in sleeves.
Join sleeve seams.

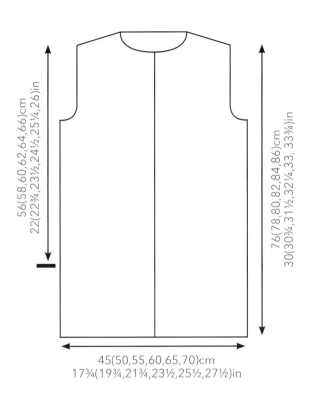

56(58,60,62,64,66)cm
22(22¾,23½,24½,25¼,26)in

76(78,80,82,84,86)cm
30(30¾,31½,32¼,33, 33¾)in

45(50,55,60,65,70)cm
17¾(19¾,21¾,23½,25½,27½)in

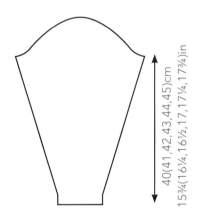

40(41,42,43,44,45)cm
15¾(16¼,16½,17,17¼,17¾)in

houndstooth jacket ...

SIZE
To fit bust

71-76	81-86	91-97	102-107	112-117	122-127	cm
28-30	32-34	36-38	40-42	44-46	48-50	in

Actual Size

98	108	119	127	138	148	cm
38½	42½	46¾	50	54¼	58¼	in

YARN
Rowan Valley Tweed
A - Malham 101

13	14	15	16	17	18	x 50gm

B- Gordale 105

13	14	15	16	17	18	x 50gm

NEEDLES
3.75mm (no 9) (US 5) needles
4.5mm (no 7) (US 7) needles

TENSION
19 stitches and 22 rows to 10cm / 4in measured over pattern using 4.5mm (US 7) needles and holding 2 strands of yarn together

EXTRAS
2 long coloured threads
8 buttons

BACK
Using 3.75mm (US 5) needles and holding 2 strands of yarn A together, cast on 95(105,115,123,133,143) sts.
Starting with a K row, work 9 rows in st st.
Next Row (WS): K to end for fold line.
Change to 4.5mm (US 7) needles.
Using 2 strands of yarn together throughout and Fair Isle technique, work colour patt as follows:
Row 1 (RS): K3(4,1,1,2,3) edge sts of row 1 of chart, K 8-st rep to last 4(5,2,2,3,4) sts, K4(5,2,2,3,4) edge sts.
Row 2: P4(5,2,2,3,4) edge sts of row 2 of chart, P 8-st rep to last 3(4,1,1,2,3) sts, P3(4,1,1,2,3) edge sts.
Row 3 to 8: Rep last 2 rows 3 times more working rows 3 to 8 of chart.
These 8 rows form patt.
Cont in patt until Back meas 71(72,73,74,75,76)cm from fold line, ending with a WS row.

Shape armholes
Cast off 6(6,7,7,8,8) sts at beg of next 2 rows. 83(93,101,109,117,127) sts.
Dec 1 st at each end of next 3(3,3,3,3,5) rows and 4(5,5,6,6,5) foll alt rows. 69(77,85,91,99,107) sts.
Cont without shaping until armholes meas 19(20,21,22,23,24)cm, ending with a WS row.

Shape shoulder
Next Row: Cast off 24(27,30,32,35,38) sts, patt to last 24(27,30,32,35,38) sts, cast off last 24(27,30,32,35,38) sts. 21(23,25,27,29,31) sts.
Cast off.

LEFT FRONT
Using 3.75mm (US 5) needles and holding 2 strands of yarn A together, cast on 31(33,39,43,45,47) sts.
Staring with a K row, work 9 rows in st st.
Next Row (WS): Cast on 64(72,76,80,88,96) sts, K to end for fold line. 95(105,115,123,133,143) sts.
Place long coloured thread in the middle of the 64(72,76,80,88,96) cast on sts and keep taking the thread back and forth every few rows to indicate vertical fold line of facing.
Change to 4.5mm (US 7) needles.
Using 2 strands of each yarn together throughout and Fair Isle technique, work colour patt as Back.
Cont in patt until Front meas 71(72,73,74,75,76)cm from fold line, ending with a WS row.

Shape armhole

Cast off 6(6,7,7,8,8) sts at beg of next (RS) row. 89(99,108,116,125,135) sts.
Dec 1 st at armhole edge of next 3(3,3,3,3,5) rows and 4(5,5,6,6,5) foll alt rows. 82(91,100,107,116,125) sts.
Cont without shaping until armhole meas 15(16,17,18,19,20)cm, ending with a WS row.

Shape neck

Row 1 (RS): Patt 29(32,35,37,40,43) sts, place locking marker here, cast off next 42(46,54,60,64,68) sts, patt to end.
Row 2: Patt 9(11,9,8,10,12) sts, P2tog, turn and work on these sts only. 10(12,10,9,11,13) sts.
Row 3: K2tog, patt to end.
Row 4: Patt to last 2 sts, P2tog.
Rep last 2 rows, once more. 6(8,6,5,7,9) sts.
Cont without shaping until Front meas same as Back to shoulder shaping, ending with a WS row.
Cast off.
With WS facing, rejoin yarn to rem 29(32,35,37,40,43) sts, P2tog and patt to end. 28(31,34,36,39,42) sts.
Next Row (RS): Patt to last 2 sts, K2tog.
Next Row: P2tog, patt to end.
Rep last 2 rows once more. 24(27,30,32,35,38) sts.
Cont without shaping until Front meas same as Back to shoulder shaping, ending with a WS row.
Cast off.
Mark front edge to indicate position of 4 buttons; first one to come 26(27,28,29,30,31)cm up from fold line, last one just below armhole shaping and rem 2 evenly spaced between.

RIGHT FRONT

Using 3.75mm (US 5) needles and holding 2 strands of yarn A together, cast on 64(72,76,80,88,96) sts and leave these sts on a spare needle.
Using 3.75mm (US 5) needles and holding 2 strands of yarn A together, cast on 31(33,39,43,45,47) sts.
Staring with a K row, work 9 rows in st st.
Next Row (WS): K to end for fold line, then K64(72,76,80,88,96) sts on spare needle. 95(105,115,123,133,143) sts.
Place long coloured thread in the middle of the 64(72,76,80,88,96) cast on sts and keep taking the thread back and forth every few rows to indicate vertical fold line of facing.
Change to 4.5mm (US 7) needles.
Using 2 strands of each yarn together throughout and Fair Isle technique, work colour patt as Back.
Cont in patt until Front meas 26(27,28,29,30,31)cm from fold line, ending with a WS row.

Buttonhole Row 1: Patt 5(5,6,6,7,7), cast off next 3 sts, patt 16(20,20,22,24,28) including st used in casting off, cast off next 3 sts, patt 10(10,12,12,14,14) including st used in casting off, cast off next 3 sts, patt 16(20,20,22,24,28) including st used in casting off, cast off next 3 sts, patt to end.

Buttonhole Row 2: Patt to end casting on 3 sts over those cast off in previous row.
Making 3 more sets of buttonholes as given above to match markers on Left Front, cont in patt until Front meas 71(72,73,74,75,76)cm, ending with a RS row.

Shape armhole
Cast off 6(6,7,7,8,8) sts at beg of next (WS) row. 89(99,108,116,125,135) sts.
Dec 1 st at armhole edge of next 3(3,3,3,3,5) rows and 4(5,5,6,6,5) foll alt rows. 82(91,100,107,116,125) sts.
Cont without shaping until armhole meas 15(16,17,18,19,20)cm, ending with a WS row.

Shape neck
Row 1 (RS): Patt 11(13,11,10,12,14) sts, cast off next 42(46,54,60,64,68) sts, place locking marker here, patt to end.
Row 2: Patt 27(30,33,35,38,41) sts, P2tog, turn and work on these 28(31,34,36,39,42) sts only.
Row 3: K2tog, patt to end.
Row 4: Patt to last 2 sts, P2tog.
Rep last 2 rows once more. 24(27,30,32,35,38) sts.
Cont without shaping until Front meas same as Back to shoulder shaping, ending with a WS row.
Cast off.
With WS facing, rejoin yarn to rem 11(13,11,10,12,14) sts, P2tog and patt to end. 10(12,10,9,11,13) sts.
Next Row (RS): Patt to last 2 sts, K2tog.
Next Row: P2tog, patt to end.
Rep last 2 rows, once more. 6(8,6,5,7,9) sts.
Cont without shaping until Front meas same as Back to shoulder shaping, ending with a WS row.
Cast off.

SLEEVES (both alike)
Using 3.75mm (US 5) needles and holding 2 strands of yarn A together, cast on 47(47,51,51,55,55) sts.
Staring with a K row, work 9 rows in st st.
Next Row (WS): K to end for fold line.
Change to 4.5mm (US 7) needles.
Working in colour patt as given for 1st(1st,3rd,3rd,1st,1st) size on Back, work 14 rows.
Inc and work into patt 1 st at each end of next row and every foll 10th(8th, 8th, 8th, 8th, 6th) row until there are 63(67,71,73,77,79) sts.
Cont without shaping until sleeve meas 44(45,46,47,48,49)cm, ending with a WS row.

Shape top
Cast off 6(6,7,7,8,8) sts at beg of next 2 rows. 51(55,57,59,61,63) sts.
Dec 1 st at each end of next row and 4(4,5,3,4,5) foll 4th rows. 41(45,45,51,51,51) sts.
Patt 1 row.
Dec 1 st at each end of next row and 4(4,3,6,4,3) foll alt rows. 31(35,37,37,41,43) sts.
Patt 1 row.
Dec 1 st at each end of next 3(5,5,5,7,7) rows. 25(25,27,27,27,29) sts.

Next Row: Cast off 3, patt to last 2 sts, work 2tog.
Rep last row, once more. 17(17,19,19,19,21) sts.
Cast off.

MAKING UP
Press as described on the information page.
On each Front, fold facing to wrong side along coloured thread, aligning neck shaping, and buttonholes on Right Front, and slip stitch in position, then join open edges at top and bottom. Neaten buttonholes. Discard colour threads.
Join both shoulder seams, using mattress stitch.

NECKBAND
With RS facing and using 3.75mm (US 5) needles, rejoin 2 strands of yarn A at marker on right front neck edge, pick up and K10 sts up right front neck edge, 27(29,31,33,35,37) sts across back neck, 10 sts down left front neck to marker. 47(49,51,53,55,57) sts.
Starting with a P row, work in st st for 9cm, ending with a K row.
Next Row: K to end for fold line.
Change to 4.5mm (US 7) needles.
Starting with a row 1 and working in colour patt as given for
1st(2nd,3rd,5th,1st,2nd) sizes on Back, work in patt until collar measures 10cm from fold line. Cast off.
Fold collar in half with wrong side inside and join side edges, then slip stitch remainder of collar to neck edge.
Sew in sleeves.
Join side and sleeve seams.
Fold facings along fold lines at lower edges and slip stitch in place.
Sew on buttons.

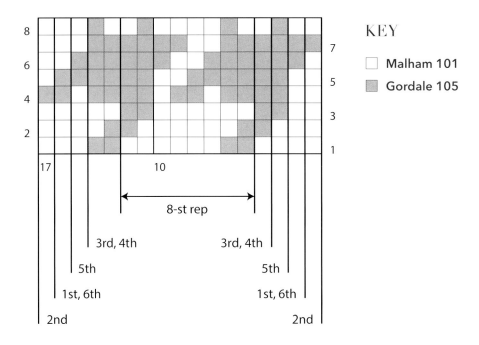

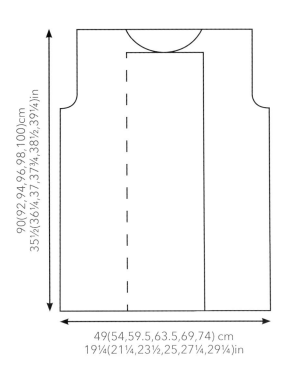

90(92,94,96,98,100)cm
35½(36¼,37,37¾,38½,39¼)in

49(54,59.5,63.5,69,74) cm
19¼(21¼,23½,25,27¼,29¼)in

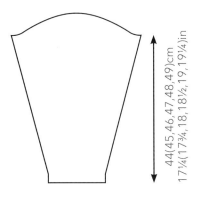

44(45,46,47,48,49)cm
17¼(17¾,18,18½,19,19¼)in

herringbone scarf ..

SIZE
30cm / 11¾in wide and 140cm / 55in long

YARN
Rowan Valley Tweed & Rowan Kidsilk Haze
A – (VT) Curlew 119
       1   x 50gm
B – (KSH) Turkish Plum 660
       1   x 25gm
C – (VT) Malham 101
       1   x 50gm
D – (KSH) Steel 664
       1   x 25gm
NEEDLES
3.25mm (no 10) (US 3) needles

TENSION
24 sts and 36 rows to 10cm / 4in measured over stocking stitch using 3.25mm
(US 3) needles holding 1 strand of Valley Tweed and 1 strand of Kidsilk Haze together

SCARF
Using 3.25mm (US 3) needles and holding yarn A and B together, cast on 72sts.
Starting with a K row, work in st st for 10 rows.
Next Row (RS): Purl.
Starting with a P row work in st st for 9 rows.
Next Row (RS): Knit across the row knitting into the cast on edge at the same time.
Next Row: Purl.
Chart rows use the Fair Isle technique, repeat 12-stitch chart 6 times across the row.
Work chart until scarf meas 137cm, ending with a WS row.
Using yarns A and B held together only, work in st st for 10 rows.
Next Row (RS): Purl.
Starting with a P row, work in st st for 9 rows.
Cast off knitwise.

FINISHING OFF
Press as described on the information page.
Join cast off edge to wrong side of work as other edge.

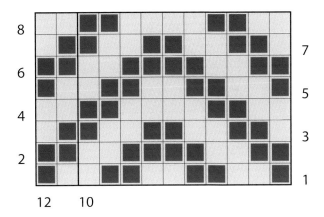

KEY

█ **Curlew 119 & Turkish Plum 660**

▫ **Malham 101 & Steel 664**

beanie ..

SIZE
Average adult head

YARN
Rowan Valley Tweed
　　　1　　x 50gm
(photographed in Calluna 116)

NEEDLES
3.25mm (no 10) (US 3) needles

TENSION
24 stitches and 38 rows to 10cm / 4in measured over pattern using 3.25mm (US 3) needles

OTHER MATERIALS
Rowan Faux Fur pompom

HAT

Using 3.25mm (US 3) needles, cast on 115 stitches.

Row 1 (RS): K1, * P1, K1, rep from * to end.

Row 2: P1, * K1, P1, rep from * to end.

Rep rows 1-2 until work measures 3cm, ending with row 2.

Work in pattern:

Row 1: (RS) K3, * P2, K2, P2, K1, P2, K2, P2, K3, rep from * to end.

Row 2: [P2, K2] twice, P3, * K2, P2, K2, P1, K2, P2, K2, P3, rep from * to last 8 sts, [K2, P2] twice.

Row 3: K2, * P1, K2, P2, K5, P2, K2, P1, K1, rep from * to last st, K1

Row 4: P4, K2, P2, K1, P1, K1, * P2, K2, P5, K2, P2, K1, P1, K1, rep from * to last 8 sts, P2, K2, P4.

Rows 1-4 form patt.

Repeat rows 1-4, 14 times more.

Shape crown

Row 1 (RS): K1, K2tog, * P2, K2, P2, K1, P2, K2, P2, sl1, K2tog, psso, rep from * to last 16 sts, P2, K2, P2, K1, P2, K2, P2, sl1, K1, psso, K1. 101 sts.

Row 2: P2, K1, * P2, K2, P3, K2, P2, K1, P1, K1, rep from * to last 14 sts, P2, K2, P3, K2, P2, K1, P2.

Row 3: K4, * P2, K5, rep from * to last 6 sts, P2, K4.

Row 4: P3, * K2, P2, K1, P1, K1, P2, K2, P3, rep from * to end.

Row 5: K1, K2tog, * P1, K2, P2, K1, P2, K2, P1, sl1, K2tog, psso, rep from * to last 14 sts, P1, K2, P2, K1, P2, K2, P1, sl1, K1, psso, K1. 87 sts.

Row 6: P4, * K2, P3, K2, P5, rep from * to last 11 sts, K2, P3, K2, P4.

Row 7: K1, K2tog, * P2, K5, P2, sl1, K2tog, psso, rep from * to last 12 sts, P2, K5, P2, sl1, K1, psso, K1. 73 sts.

Row 8: [P2, K1] twice, * P1, K1, P2, K1, rep from * to last 2 sts, P2.

Row 9: K1, K2tog, K1,* [P2, K1] twice, sl1, K2tog, psso, K1, rep from * to last 9 sts, [P2, K1] twice, sl1, K1, psso, K1. 59 sts.

Row 10: P2, K2, * P3, K2, P1, K2, rep from * to last 7 sts, P3, K2, P2.

Row 11: K1, K2tog, * K5, sl1, K2tog, psso, rep from * to last 8 sts, K5, sl1, K1, psso, K1. 45 sts.

Row 12: P3, * K1, P1, K1, P3, rep from * to end.

Row 13: K1, K2tog, * P1, K1, P1, sl1, K2tog, psso, rep from * to last 6 sts, P1, K1, P1, sl1, K1, psso, K1. 31 sts.

Row 14: P to end.

Row 15: K1, K2tog, * K1, sl1, K2tog, psso, rep from * to last 4 sts, K1, sl1, K1, psso, K1. 17 sts.

Row 16: P1, * P2tog, rep from * to end. 9 sts.

Break off yarn and thread end through remaining sts pull up tightly and fasten off.

MAKING UP

Press as described on the information page.

Join back seam using mattress stitch. Attach pompom to top of hat.

snood ..

SIZE
54cm / 21¼in circumference and 49cm / 19¼in long

YARN
Rowan Valley Tweed

     3   x 50gm

(photographed in Calluna 116)

NEEDLES
3.25mm (no 10) (US 3) circular needle, 60cm long – if worked in round
3.25mm (no 10) (US 3) needles – if worked flat
Cable needle

TENSION
40 stitches and 36 rounds to 10cm / 4in measured over cable pattern
using 3.25mm (US 3) needles

SPECIAL ABBREVIATIONS
C8B, cable 8 back (sl next 4 sts onto cable needle and leave at back
of work, K4, then K4 from cable needle)
C8F, cable 8 front (sl next 4 sts onto cable needle and leave at front
of work, K4, then K4 from cable needle)

SNOOD (worked in round)
Using 3.25mm circular needle, cast on 216 sts.
Making sure that the cast-on edge is not twisted, join in the rnd placing marker for beg of rnd.
Rnd 1: *K1, P1, rep from * to end.
Rep rnd 1, 9 times more.
Work in cable pattern:
Rnds 1-4: * K8, P1, rep from * to end.
Rnd 5: * C8B, P1, C8F, P1, rep from * to end.
Rnds 6-8: * K8, P1, rep from * to end.
Rnds 1-8 form cable patt.
Cont in patt until work measures 46cm, ending with rnd 3.
Next Rnd: * K1, P1, rep from * to end.
Rep last rnd 9 times more.
Cast off loosely in rib.

MAKING UP
Press as described on the information page.

SNOOD (worked flat)
Using 3.25mm (US3) circular needle, cast on 218 sts.
Making sure that the cast-on edge is not twisted, work in rows as follows:
Row 1: K2, * P1, K1, rep from * to end.
Rep row 1, 9 times more.
Work in cable pattern:
Row 1 (RS): K1, * K8, P1, rep from * to last st, K1.
Row 2: P1, * K1, P8, rep from * to last st, P1.
Rows 3-4: Rep rows 1-2 once more.
Row 5: K1, * C8B, P1, C8F, P1, rep from * to last st, K1
Row 6: As row 2
Rows 7-8: Rep rows 1-2 once more
Rows 1 to 8 form cable patt.
Cont in patt until work measures 46cm, ending with row 4.
Next Row: K2, * P1, K1, rep from * to end.
Rep last row 9 times more.
Cast off loosely in rib.

MAKING UP
Press as described on the information page.
Join side edges with mattress stitch.

roll neck jumper •

SIZE

To fit bust

71-76	81-86	91-97	102-107	112-117	122-127	cm
28-30	32-34	36-38	40-42	44-46	48-50	in

Actual Size

94	108	118	127	136	146	cm
37	42½	46½	50	53½	57½	in

YARN

Rowan Valley Tweed and Rowan Kidsilk Haze

VT – Penyghent 104

7	8	8	9	10	10	x 50gm

KSH – Smoke 605

14	15	16	18	19	20	x 25gm

NEEDLES

5mm (no 6) (US 8) needles

TENSION
17 stitches and 22 rows to 10cm / 4in measured over stocking stitch using 5mm (US 8) needles and holding 2 strands of Valley Tweed and 1 strand of Kidsilk Haze together

EXTRAS
Stitch Holders

BACK
Using 5mm needles and holding 2 strands of Valley Tweed and 1 strand of Kidsilk Haze together throughout, cast on 82(94,102,110,118,126) sts.
Row 1: (RS) K2, * P2, K2, rep from * to end.
Row 2: P2, * K2, P2, rep from * to end.
Rows 1 and 2 form rib.
Cont in rib until Back measures 10cm, ending with a WS row.
Starting with a K row, work in st st until Back measures 45(46,47,48,49,50)cm, ending with WS row.

Shape armholes
Cast off 3(4,4,4,4,4) sts at beg of next 2 rows. 76(86,94,102,110,118) sts.
Dec 1 st at each end of next 3(3,3,4,4,5) rows. 70(80,88,94,102,108) sts. **
Cont without shaping until armholes measure 22(23,23,24,24,25)cm, ending with a WS row.

Shape shoulders
Next Row: Cast off 19(24,28,30,34,37) sts, K to last 19(24,28,30,34,37) sts, cast off last 19(24,28,30,34,37) sts.
Leave rem 32(32,32,34,34,34) sts on a st holder.

FRONT
Work as Back to **
Cont without shaping until armholes measure 14(15,15,16,16,17)cm, ending with a WS row.

Shape neck
Next Row (RS): K26(31,35,37,41,44), turn and work on these sts only.
Dec 1 st at neck edge on next 3 rows and 4 foll alt rows. 19(24,28,30,34,37) sts.
Cont without shaping until armhole measures 22(23,23,24,24,25)cm, ending with a WS row.
Cast off.
With right side facing, slip centre 18(18,18,20,20,20) sts onto st holder, rejoin yarn to rem sts and K to end. 26(31,35,37,41,44) sts.
 Dec 1 st at neck edge on next 3 rows and 4 foll alt rows. 19(24,28,30,34,37) sts.
Cont without shaping until armholes measure 22(23,23,24,24,25)cm, ending with a WS row.
Cast off.

SLEEVES (both alike)
Using 5mm (US 8) needles and holding 2 strands of Valley Tweed and 1 strand of Kidsilk Haze together throughout, cast on 42(42,46,46,50,50) sts.
Row 1: (RS) K2, * P2, K2, rep from * to end.
Row 2: P2, * K2, P2, rep from * to end.
Rows 1 and 2 form rib.
Cont in rib until sleeve measures 10cm, ending with a WS row.
Starting with a K row, work 4 rows in st st.
Cont in st st and inc 1 st at each end of next row, 6(11,4,9,2,8) following 4th rows, then on every foll 6th rows until there are 64(68,68,72,72,76) sts.
Cont without shaping until sleeve measure 43(44,45,46,47,48)cm, ending with a WS row.

Shape top
Cast off 3(4,4,4,4,4) sts at beg of next 2 rows. 58(60,60,64,64,68) sts.
Dec 1 st at each end of next 3(3,3,4,4,5) rows. 52(54,54,56,56,58) sts.
Next Row: Cast off 6, work to last 2 sts, work 2tog.
Rep last row 3 times more. 24(26,26,28,28,30) sts.
Cast off.

MAKING UP
Press as described on the information page.
Join right-shoulder seam using mattress stitch.
Collar
With right side facing, using 5mm (US 8) needles and holding 2 strands of Valley Tweed and 1 strand of Kidsilk Haze together throughout, pick up and K19 sts down Left Front neck, work across st on Front st holder as follows: K2(2,2,4,4,4), [inc K wise in next st, K3] 4 times, pick up and K19 sts up Right Front neck, work across sts at Back st holder as follows: K3(3,3,4,4,4), [inc K wise in next st, K4] 5 times, inc K wise in next st, K3(3,3,4,4,4).
98(98,98,102,102,102) sts.
Row 1 (WS): P2, * K2, P2, rep from * to end.
Row 2: K2, * P2, K2, rep from * to end.
Rows 1 and 2 form rib.
Cont in rib until collar measures 20cm.
Cast off loosely in rib.
Join left-shoulder and polo-collar seams, reversing seam half way up on collar for turn back. Sew in sleeves. Join side and sleeve seams.

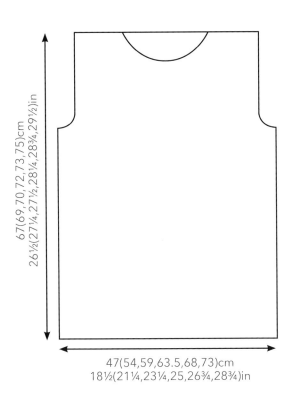

67(69,70,72,73,75)cm
26½(27¼,27½,28¼,28¾,29½)in

47(54,59,63.5,68,73)cm
18½(21¼,23¼,25,26¾,28¾)in

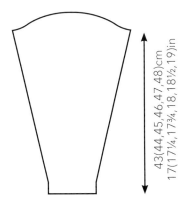

43(44,45,46,47,48)cm
17(17¼,17¾,18,18½,19)in

cable detail jumper ..

SIZE
To fit bust

71-76	81-86	91-97	102-107	112-117	122-127	cm
28-30	32-34	36-38	40-42	44-46	48-50	in

Actual Size

121	131	141	151	161	171	cm
47¾	51½	55½	59½	63½	67¼	in

YARN
Rowan Valley Tweed

8	9	9	10	10	11	x 50gm

(photographed in Curlew 119)

NEEDLES
3.25mm (no 10) (US 3) needles (You will needle long needles or circular).
Cable needle

TENSION

24 stitches and 36 rows to 10cm / 4in measured over stocking stitch using 3.25mm (US 3) needles
28-stitch cable panel measures 9.5cm / 3¾in across using 3.25mm (US 3) needles

EXTRAS

Stitch Holders

SPECIAL ABBREVIATIONS

C3f, cable 3 front (sl next 2 sts onto cable needle and leave at front of work, K1, then K2 from cable needle)
C4f, cable 4 front (sl next 2 sts onto cable needle and leave at front of work, K2, then K2 from cable needle)
C4b, cable 4 back (sl next 2 sts onto cable needle and leave at back of work, K2, then K2 from cable needle)
Cr3lt, cross 3 left (sl next 2 sts onto cable needle and leave at front of work, P1, then K2 from cable needle)
Cr3rt, cross 3 right (sl next st onto cable needle and leave at back of work, K2, then P1 from cable needle)

CABLE PANEL

Worked over 28 sts.
Row 1 (RS): P2, K3, [P1, K1] 4 times, P1, C4f, K1, P1, K2, P6.
Row 2: K6, P2, K1, P5, K1, [P1, K1] 4 times, P3, K2.
Row 3: P2, Cr3lt, [K1, P1] 4 times, Cr3rt, Cr3lt, Cr3rt, P6.
Row 4: K7, P4, K2, P2, K1, [P1, K1] 3 times, P3, K3.
Row 5: P3, Cr3lt, [K1, P1] 3 times, Cr3rt, P2, C4b, P7.
Row 6: K7, P4, K3, P2, K1, [P1, K1] twice, P3, K4.
Row 7: P4, Cr3lt, [K1, P1] twice, Cr3rt, P2, Cr3rt, C3f, P6.
Row 8: K6, P3, K1, P2, K3, P2, K1, P1, K1, P3, K5.
Row 9: P5, Cr3lt, K1, P1, Cr3rt, P2, Cr3rt, K1, P1, C3f, P5.
Row 10: K5, P3, K1, P1, K1, P2, K3, P2, K1, P3, K6.
Row 11: P6, Cr3lt, Cr3rt, P2, Cr3rt, [K1, P1] twice, C3f, P4.
Row 12: K4, P3, K1, [P1, K1] twice, P2, K3, P4, K7.
Row 13: P7, C4b, P2, Cr3rt, [K1, P1] 3 times, C3f, P3.
Row 14: K3, P3, K1, [P1, K1] 3 times, P2, K2, P4, K7.
Row 15: P6, Cr3rt, C3f, Cr3rt, [K1, P1] 4 times, C3f, P2.
Row 16: K2, P3, K1, [P1, K1] 4 times, P5, K1, P2, K6.
Row 17: P6, K3, P1, C4f, [K1, P1] 5 times, K2, P2.
Row 18: K2, P2, K1, [P1, K1] 4 times, P5, K1, P3, K6.
Row 19: P6, Cr3lt, Cr3rt, Cr3lt, [K1, P1] 4 times, Cr3rt, P2.
Row 20: K3, P2, K1, [P1, K1] 3 times, P3, K2, P4, K7.
Row 21: P7, C4b, P2, Cr3lt, [K1, P1] 3 times, Cr3rt, P3.
Row 22: K4, P2, K1, [P1, K1] twice, P3, K3, P4, K7.
Row 23: P6, Cr3rt, C3f, P2, Cr3lt, [K1, P1] twice, Cr3rt, P4.
Row 24: K5, P2, K1, P1, K1, P3, K3, P3, K1, P2, K6.
Row 25: P5, Cr3rt, K1, P1, C3f, P2, Cr3lt, K1, P1, Cr3rt, P5.
Row 26: K6, P2, K1, P3, K3, P3, K1, P1, K1, P2, K5.
Row 27: P4, Cr3rt, [K1, P1] twice, C3f, P2, Cr3lt, Cr3rt, P6.
Row 28: K7, P4, K3, P3, K1, [P1, K1] twice, P2, K4.
Row 29: P3, Cr3rt, [K1, P1] 3 times, C3f, P2, C4b, P7.
Row 30: K7, P4, K2, P3, K1, [P1, K1] 3 times, P2, K3.
Row 31: P2, Cr3rt, [K1, P1] 4 times, C3f, Cr3rt, C3f, P6.

Row 32: K6, P3, K1, P5, K1, [P1, K1] 4 times, P2, K2.
These 32 rows form cable panel.

BACK
Using 3.25mm (US 3) needles, cast on 145(157,169,181,193,205) sts.
Piece is worked flat. If using circular needle, do not join in the round.
Row 1 (RS): K1, * P1, K1, rep from * to end.
Row 2: P1, * K1, P1, rep from * to end.
Rows 1 and 2 form rib.
Cont in rib until Back meas 8cm, ending with a RS row.
Next Row (WS): Rib 15(17,19,21,23,25), [inc in next st, rib 2] 5 times, inc in next st, rib 83(91,99,107,115,123), [inc in next st, rib 2] 5 times, inc in next st, rib to end. 157(169,181,193,205,217) sts.
Work patt:
Row 1: K12(14,16,18,20,22), work row 1 of cable panel, K77(85,93,101,109,117), work row 1 of cable panel, K to end.
Row 2: P12(14,16,18,20,22), work row 2 of cable panel, P77(85,93,101,109,117), work row 2 of cable panel, P to end.
Rows 3-32: Rep rows 1-2 another 15 times working rows 3 to 32 of cable panel.
Rows 1 to 32 form patt.
Work in patt until Back meas 46(46,48,48,50,50)cm, ending with WS row.
Mark each end of last row. **
Cont in patt until Back meas 20(21,22,23,24,25)cm from markers, ending with a WS row.

Shape shoulders
Cast off 12(14,16,18,20,22) sts at beg of next 2 rows. 133(141,149,157,165,173) sts.
Next Row: Cast off 14 sts but working patt 2, [work 2tog, patt 2] 3 times across these 14 sts, patt to end.
Rep last row 3 times more. 77(85,93,101,109,117) sts.
Cast off 8(10,11,12,13,15) sts at beg of next 2 rows and 8(9,10,12,14,15) sts at beg of foll 2 rows.
Leave rem 45(47,51,53,55,57) sts on a st holder.

FRONT
Work as for Back to **.
Cont in patt until Front meas 14(15,16,17,18,19)cm from markers, ending with a WS row.

Shape neck
Next Row (RS): Patt 64(69,73,78,83,88), turn and work on these sts only.
Dec 1 st at neck edge on next 8 rows. 56(61,65,70,75,80) sts.
Cont without shaping until Front meas same as Back to shoulder shaping, ending with a WS row.

Shape shoulder
Cast off 12(14,16,18,20,22) sts at beg of next row. 44(47,49,52,55,58) sts.
Work 1 row.
Next Row (RS): Cast off 14 sts but working patt 2, [K2tog, patt 2] 3 times across these 14 sts, patt to end.
Work 1 row.

Rep last 2 rows once more. 16(19,21,24,27,30) sts.
Cast off 8(10,11,12,13,15) sts at beg of next row. 8(9,10,12,14,15) sts.
Work 1 row.
Cast off.
With right side facing, slip centre 29(31,35,37,39,41) sts onto st holder, rejoin yarn to rem sts and patt to end. 64(69,73,78,83,88) sts.
Dec 1 st at neck edge on next 8 rows. 56(61,65,70,75,80) sts.
Cont without shaping until Front meas same as Back to shoulder shaping, ending with a RS row.

Shape shoulder
Cast off 12(14,16,18,20,22) sts at beg of next row. 44(47,49,52,55,58) sts.
Work 1 row.
Next Row (WS): Cast off 14 sts but working patt 2, [P2tog, patt 2] 3 times across these 14 sts, patt to end.
Work 1 row.
Reap last 2 rows once more. 16(19,21,24,27,30) sts.
Cast off 8(10,11,12,13,15) sts at beg of next row. 8(9,10,12,14,15) sts.
Work 1 row.
Cast off.

SLEEVES (both alike)
Using 3.25mm (US 3) needles, cast on 45(45,49,49,55,55) sts.
Row 1: (RS) K1, * P1, K1, rep from * to end.
Row 2: P1, * K1, P1, rep from * to end.
Rows 1 and 2 form rib.
Cont in rib until sleeve measures 8cm, ending with a RS row.
Next Row (WS): Inc in first st, rib 13(13,15,15,18,18), [inc in next st, rib 3] 4 times, inc in next st, rib to last st, inc in last st.
52(52,56,56,62,62) sts.
Work patt:
Row 1: K12(12,14,14,17,17), work row 1 of cable panel, K to end.
Row 2: P12(12,14,14,17,17), work row 2 of cable panel, P to end.
Rows 1 and 2 set position of cable panel.
Keeping panel correct and working inc sts into st st, inc 1 st at each end of
3rd row and 4(6,7,9,9,11) foll alt rows then on every foll 4th row until there are
102(106,112,116,122,126) sts.
Cont without shaping until sleeve measures 39(40,41,42,43,44)cm, ending with WS row.
Cast off but working [work 2 tog, patt 2] 7 times across 28 sts of cable panel.

MAKING UP
Press as described on the information page.
Join right shoulder seam using mattress stitch.

Neckband
With right side facing and using 3.25mm (US 3) needles, pick up and K17 sts down Left Front neck, K29(31,35,37,39,41) sts on Front st holder, pick up and K17 sts up Right Front neck, K45(47,51,53,55,57) sts on Back st holder inc 1 st at centre.
109(113,121,125,129,133) sts.
Row 1: P1, * K1, P1, rep from * to end.
Row 2: K1, * P1, K1, rep from * to end.
Rows 1 and 2 form rib.
Cont in rib until neckband measures 8cm.
Cast off in rib.
Join left shoulder and neckband seam. Sew on sleeve tops between markers on side edges of back and front. Join side and sleeve seams.

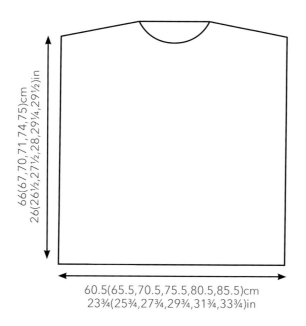

66(67,70,71,74,75)cm
26(26½,27½,28,29¼,29½)in

60.5(65.5,70.5,75.5,80.5,85.5)cm
23¾(25¾,27¾,29¾,31¾,33¾)in

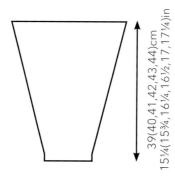

39(40,41,42,43,44)cm
15¼(15¾,16¼,16½,17,17¼)in

EXPERIENCE RATING

for guidance only

● BEGINNER TECHNIQUES

For the beginner knitter, basic garment shaping and straight forward stitch technique.

● ● SIMPLE TECHNIQUES

Simple straight forward knitting, introducing various, shaping techniques and garments.

● ● ● EXPERIENCE TECHNIQUES

For the more experienced knitter, using more advanced shaping techniques at the same time as colourwork or more advanced stitch techniques.

● ● ● ● ADVANCED TECHNIQUES

Advanced techniques used, using advanced stitches and garment shaping along with more challenging techniques.

SIZING

To help you enjoy a great knitting experience and a well fitting garment please refer to our sizing guide which conforms to standard clothing sizes. Dimensions in our sizing guide are body measurements, not garment dimensions, please refer to the size diagram for this measurement.

SIZING GUIDE

UK SIZE	XS	S	M	L	XL	XXL	
To fit bust	28 – 30	32 – 34	36 – 38	40 – 42	44 – 46	44 – 46	inches
	71 – 76	81 – 86	91 – 97	102 – 107	112 – 117	122 – 127	cm
To fit waist	20 – 22	24 – 26	28 – 30	32 – 34	36 – 38	40 – 42	inches
	51 – 56	61 – 66	71 – 76	81 – 86	91 – 97	102 – 107	cm
To fit hips	30 – 31	34 – 36	38 – 40	42 – 44	46 – 48	50 – 52	inches
	76 – 81	86 – 91	97 – 102	107 – 112	117 – 122	127 – 132	cm

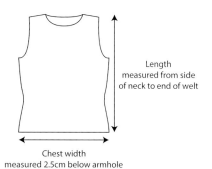

SIZING & SIZE DIAGRAM NOTE

The instructions are given for the smallest size. Where they vary, work the figures in brackets for the larger sizes. One set of figures refers to all sizes. Included with most patterns in this magazine is a 'size diagram' - see image on the right, of the finished garment and its dimensions. The measurement shown at the bottom of each 'size diagram' shows the garment width 2.5cm below the armhole shaping. To help you choose the size of garment to knit please refer to the sizing guide. Generally in the majority of designs the welt width (at the cast on edge of the garment) is the same width as the chest. However, some designs may be 'A-Line' in shape or flared edge and in these cases welt width will be wider than the chest width.

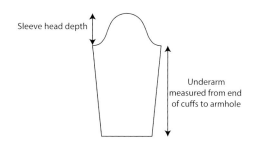

Length measured from side of neck to end of welt

Chest width measured 2.5cm below armhole

Sleeve head depth

Underarm measured from end of cuffs to armhole

MEASURING GUIDE

For maximum comfort and to ensure the correct fit when choosing a size to knit, please follow the tips below when checking your size. Measure yourself close to your body, over your underwear and don't pull the tape measure too tight!

Bust/chest – measure around the fullest part of the bust/chest and across the shoulder blades.

Waist – measure around the natural waistline, just above the hip bone.

Hips – measure around the fullest part of the bottom.

If you don't wish to measure yourself, note the size of a favourite jumper that you like the fit of. Our sizes are now comparable to the clothing sizes from the major high street retailers, so if your favourite jumper is a size Medium or size 12, then our Medium should be approximately the same fit. To be extra sure, measure your favourite jumper and then compare these measurements with the Rowan size diagram given at the end of the individual instructions.

Finally, once you have decided which size is best for you, please ensure that you achieve the tension required for the design you wish to knit.

Remember if your tension is too loose, your garment will be bigger than the pattern size and you may use more yarn. If your tension is too tight, your garment could be smaller than the pattern size and you will have yarn left over.

Furthermore if your tension is incorrect, the handle of your fabric will be too stiff or floppy and will not fit properly. It really does make sense to check your tension before starting every project.

PHOTOGRAPHY MODEL SIZING
The models used in this collection wear a UK dress size 8 and 10. Wearing garments that were knitted in a size Small. Height: 173cm / 5ft 8in

ABBREVIATIONS

alt	alternate
beg	begin(ning)
cm	centimetres
cont	continue
C4F	slip next 2 stitches onto a cable needle and hold in front of work, knit next 2 stitches, knit 2 stitches from cable needle.
C4B	slip next 2 stitches onto a cable needle and hold at back of work, know next 2 stitches, knit 2 stitches from cable needle.
dec	decrease(s)(ing)
foll(s)	follow(s)(ing)
g	grams
g st	garter stitch (knit all rows)
in	inch(es)
inc	increase(s)(ing)
K	knit
Kfb	knit in front and back of stitch (makes 1stitch)
M1	make 1 stitch
meas	measures
mm	millimetres
P	purl
patt	pattern
psso	pass slipped stitch over
rem	remain(ing)
rep	repeat
RS	right side of work
Sl 1	slip 1 stitch
st st	stocking stitch (knit on RS rows, purl on WS rows)
st(s)	stitch(es)
tbl	through back of loop
tog	together
WS	wrong side of work

TENSION

This is the size of your knitting. Most of the knitting patterns will have a tension quoted. This is how many stitches 10cm/4in in width and how many rows 10cm/4in in length to make a square. If your knitting doesn't match this then your finished garment will not measure the correct size. To obtain the correct measurements for your garment you must achieve the tension.

The tension quoted on a ball band is the manufacturer's average. For the manufacturer and designers to produce designs they have to use a tension for you to be able to obtain the measurements quoted. It's fine not to be the average, but you need to know if you meet the average or not. Then you can make the necessary adjustments to obtain the correct measurements.

CHOOSING YARN

All the colours and textures, where do you start? Look for the thickness, how chunky do you want your finished garment? Sometimes it's colour that draws you to a yarn or perhaps you have a pattern that requires a specific yarn. Check the washing/care instructions before you buy.

Yarn varies in thickness; there are various descriptions such as DK and 4ply these are examples of standard weights. There are a lot of yarns available that are not standard and it helps to read the ball band to see what the recommended needle size is.

This will give you an idea of the approximate thickness. It is best to use the yarn recommended in the pattern.
Keep one ball band from each project so that you have a record of what you have used and most importantly how to care for your garment after it has been completed. Always remember to give the ball band with the garment if it is a gift.

The ball band normally provides you with the average tension and recommended needle sizes for the yarn, this may vary from what has been used in the pattern, always go with the pattern as the designer may change needles to obtain a certain look. The ball band also tells you the name of the yarn and what it is made of, the weight and approximate length of the ball of yarn along with the shade and dye lot numbers. This is important as dye lots can vary, you need to buy your yarn with matching dye lots.

PRESSING AND AFTERCARE

Having spent so long knitting your project it can be a great shame not to look after it properly. Some yarns are suitable for pressing once you have finished to improve the look of the fabric. To find out this information you will need to look on the yarn ball band, where there will be washing and care symbols.

Once you have checked to see if your yarn is suitable to be pressed and the knitting is a smooth texture (stocking stitch for example), pin out and place a damp cloth onto the knitted pieces. Hold the steam iron (at the correct temperature) approximately 10cm/4in away from the fabric and steam. Keep the knitted pieces pinned in place until cool.

As a test it is a good idea to wash your tension square in the way you would expect to wash your garment.